BE YOUR ★
BEST
★ YOU ⚡

BE WELL!

A HERO'S GUIDE TO A HEALTHY MIND AND BODY

ELSIE OLSON

Consulting Editor, Diane Craig, M.A./Reading Specialist

Super Sandcastle

An Imprint of Abdo Publishing
abdobooks.com

abdobooks.com

Published by Abdo Publishing, a division of ABDO, PO Box 398166, Minneapolis, Minnesota 55439. Copyright © 2020 by Abdo Consulting Group, Inc. International copyrights reserved in all countries. No part of this book may be reproduced in any form without written permission from the publisher. Super SandCastle™ is a trademark and logo of Abdo Publishing.

Printed in the United States of America, North Mankato, Minnesota
052019
092019

THIS BOOK CONTAINS
RECYCLED MATERIALS

Design: Sarah DeYoung, Mighty Media, Inc.
Production: Mighty Media, Inc.
Editor: Jessica Rusick
Cover Photographs: iStockphoto; Shutterstock Images
Interior Photographs: iStockphoto; Mighty Media, Inc.; Shutterstock Images

Library of Congress Control Number: 2018966948

Publisher's Cataloging-in-Publication Data
Names: Olson, Elsie, author.
Title: Be well!: a hero's guide to a healthy mind and body / by Elsie Olson
Other title: A hero's guide to a healthy mind and body
Description: Minneapolis, Minnesota : Abdo Publishing, 2020 | Series: Be your best you
Identifiers: ISBN 9781532119699 (lib. bdg.) | ISBN 9781532174452 (ebook)
Subjects: LCSH: Mindfulness (Psychology)--Juvenile literature. | Children--Health and hygiene--Juvenile
    literature. | Wellness--Juvenile literature. | Child health habits--Juvenile literature. | Heroism--
    Juvenile literature. | Self-confidence in children--Juvenile literature.
Classification: DDC 372.37--dc23

Super SandCastle™ books are created by a team of professional educators, reading specialists, and content developers around five essential components—phonemic awareness, phonics, vocabulary, text comprehension, and fluency—to assist young readers as they develop reading skills and strategies and increase their general knowledge. All books are written, reviewed, and leveled for guided reading, early reading intervention, and Accelerated Reader™ programs for use in shared, guided, and independent reading and writing activities to support a balanced approach to literacy instruction.

CONTENTS

BE YOUR BEST YOU!

Do you go outside to run and play? And eat your veggies every day?

Do you take some time to clear your mind? And treat yourself in a way that's kind?

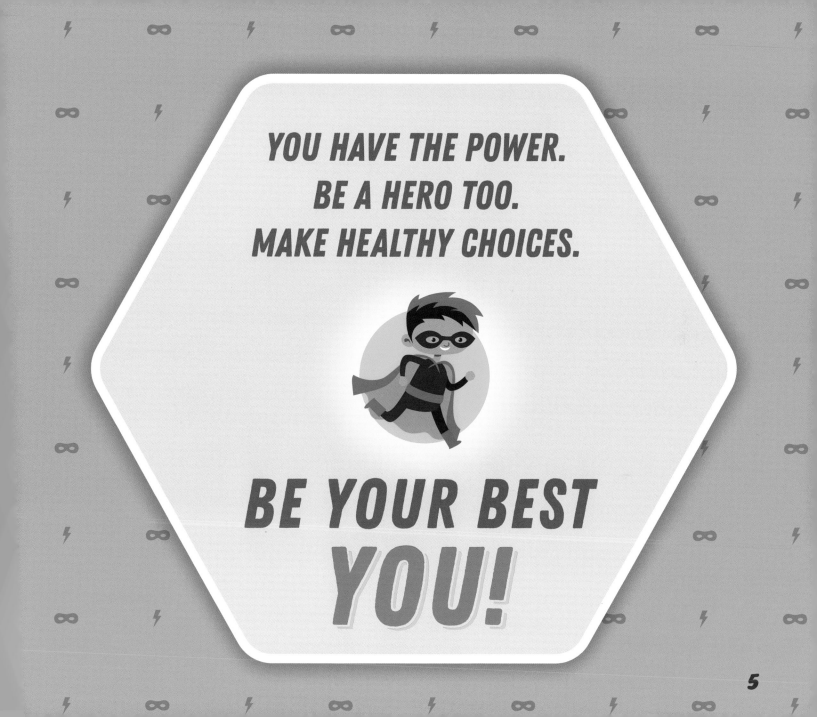

YOU HAVE THE POWER.
BE A HERO TOO.
MAKE HEALTHY CHOICES.

BE YOUR BEST YOU!

WHAT IS WELLNESS?

Being well means you are in good health. Well people take good care of their bodies. They eat healthy foods. They exercise. Wellness means having a healthy mind too!

Are You Well?

- Do you eat healthy foods?
- Do you exercise?
- Do you get enough sleep?
- Do you spend time away from screens every day?
- Do you talk to a trusted adult when you feel sad or angry?

These are signs of wellness!

HEALTHY BODY, HEALTHY MIND!

Mental health is a big part of wellness. It affects how you think, feel, and act.

Building healthy habits takes practice. But you have the superpowers to be well! Use them to build a healthy body and healthy mind.

THINK GOOD THOUGHTS!

People with healthy minds are kind to others. But they are also kind to themselves.

So think kind thoughts about yourself!

9

SUPERPOWER!
EAT WELL

Food powers your body. Eating healthfully is a great superpower! Healthy foods are **nutritious**. They give you energy to run and play!

YOU ARE WHAT YOU EAT!

Choose foods from the five healthy food groups. Here is what should go on your plate each day!

FRUITS:
1 TO 1½ CUPS

VEGGIES:
1½ CUPS

DAIRY:
2½ CUPS

GRAINS:
5 OUNCES

PROTEIN:
4 OUNCES

Drink well, too. Juice and soda have lots of sugar. Drink more water and milk.

MOVE YOUR BODY

Superheroes don't stand still. Exercise is a superpower! Find ways to be active for one hour every single day. Any movement counts!

If you sweat, you're doing it right. Just don't forget to drink lots of water!

THREE TYPES OF MOVEMENT

Stay healthy by practicing:

STRENGTH

EXAMPLE: CLIMBING THE MONKEY BARS. (THESE ACTIVITIES MAKE YOU STRONGER!)

ENDURANCE

EXAMPLE: PLAYING SOCCER. (THESE ACTIVITIES HELP YOU MOVE FOR LONGER!)

FLEXIBILITY

EXAMPLE: TOUCHING YOUR TOES. (THESE ACTIVITIES HELP YOU MOVE EASILY!)

CATCH SOME ZZZZs

Superheroes need to rest. Sleep is an important superpower!

Sleep helps keep you from getting sick. Sleep also gives your brain a break. A well-rested brain learns better.

SLEEPY TIME!

Most kids need nine to twelve hours of sleep each night.

Zzzzzzz...

MINDFULNESS

Mindfulness means paying attention to the way you think and feel. It helps keep your brain well!

Mindful people still get sad and mad. But they don't make poor choices when they feel this way.

ALL KINDS OF BRAINS

Everyone's brain works a little differently. That makes us special! Heroes have all kinds of brains.

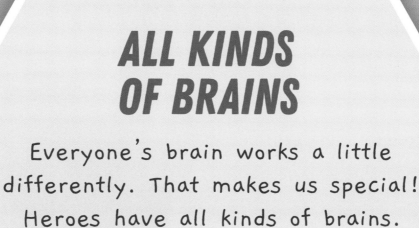

So show kindness to people who think differently from you!

BREATHING

All heroes are **anxious** sometimes. This means feeling nervous or worried. Use a superpower to calm down. Just breathe!

When you feel **stressed**, close your eyes. Breathe slowly. Soon you will feel better.

GLITTER JAR

A glitter jar can help when you feel worried! This is a jar filled with liquid and glitter. Shake the jar. Watch the glitter float. Try not to think of anything else. This can help you clear your mind.

Make your own glitter jar!

Put glitter glue and loose glitter in a jar of water. Seal the lid tightly. Shake it well.

UNPLUG AND GO OUTSIDE

Kids spend lots of time looking at screens. This includes phones, tablets, TVs, and computers. Screens are great tools for fun and learning. But it's important to give eyes a rest from screens.

Heroes know it's a good idea to take a tech break sometimes.

BE A HERO! ⭐⚡

It's your turn to take a stand. Act like a hero. Lend a hand.

With the words you say and the things you do, make healthy choices. Be your best you!

WHAT WOULD YOU DO?

Being a hero is about making healthy choices. How would you use your superpowers in the situations below?

You are thirsty, and there is soda or water to drink.

You are watching TV and a friend asks you to go on a bike ride.

Tomorrow is the first day of school, and you are too nervous to sleep.

GLOSSARY

anxious – feeling nervous or worried.

mental – relating to the mind.

mindfulness – being aware of your thoughts and feelings. People who practice mindfulness are mindful.

nutritious – good for people to eat.

stressed – to feel emotional strain or pressure.

ONLINE RESOURCES

Booklinks
NONFICTION NETWORK
FREE! ONLINE NONFICTION RESOURCES

To learn more about being well and caring for your mind and body, visit **abdobooklinks.com** or scan this QR code. These links are routinely monitored and updated to provide the most current information available.